GIRL BRED FROM
THE 90'S

Girl Bred From The 90's

Olivia Delgado

Querencia Press, LLC
Chicago, Illinois

QUERENCIA PRESS

LIBRARY OF CONGRESS CATALOGING-IN-PUBLICATION DATA

ISBN 978 1 959118 03 9

www.querenciapress.com

First Published in 2022

Querencia Press, LLC
Chicago IL

Printed & Bound in the United States of America

"It runs. Youth rolling into decades, wild and dizzying like the spell of seasons."

CONTENTS

Girlhood

We left our innocence in mud pies, jars of spring preserved for adornment on dewy stoned skies that twirled. The scope of canals traced when summer was a season left to hoard. A bevy of dandelion weeds combed to our doily sleeved forecasts when we were little girls. The clouds could shake and still we'd land safely because we knew no etiquette to playing pretend.

Digestible

You're just some portrait of a girl bred from the 90's

she doesn't know how to exist.

If lucky enough, we all become arched silhouettes sifting through piles of yesterdays. Wrapped gowns lingering at the floor in puddles of snowy needle point. Tiny drawers with aged letters and trinkets conversing in their own language. They'll eventually study the etymology of the decades we began from. Paper chain-linked garland tying us to the generations we've outgrown. Our hair gray, white disco lights.
Everything is spinning.
As kids our feet knew the fit of roller skates in December as glow stick necklaces dotted the skating rink like fireflies. We were neon.

June

I saw lightening dash across the ground and felt like a kid again.
Funny how we string remarks as charms, flying about our
memories. Last summer I imagined the dust from historic
dwellings palpable on skin. How Eastman Johnson's "In the
Fields" endured like a pattern. The way the purple-blue
plumbagoes curled into Pearl's fur after she ran through the
yard. On walks I stare at the trees and the way they dip in
luminism. I can hear summer develop a year later.
**

A school bus breezed by us and my nephew, in awe, said "Big
truck, wow!."

La Luz in Every Phase

"Don't fall too loudly, you'll wake the others." There's an air about this room, a quiver in this place. Ten years from then to here, I'm lying asleep drowning awake.

*

Fortune Telling Roads and Branded Regions:

It swayed, fading into the gloom of dusk. White marbled origami clouds, cherry mixed. Pastoral tints burning edges into the thumbprint landscape through passing windows. Evening creases draped in coastal plains, smudging hushed roads, beneath angel sky. A woman once read my palm, and I suppose if you look closely everything revisited leads back to light.

*

The Drive-In:

The sun preached that evening. Fables, tea stained and ironed in evergreen calligraphy.

Cyclical to be in the house where we were once held and comforted as kids. Twenty-five years later I'm rocking my three-month-old nephew in the very same home. Somehow, we're always pulled back. The local drive-in closed years ago. We went two times in the 90's. I remember the four of us sitting on the front of the car, backs leaning against the windshield. Young girls enveloped by the resplendent avalanche of celestial sparks glowing above. The screen spread wide in front of us lying atop a dried lot. Pebbled dirt and lunar landings commingling on our skin. We already knew too much. Knew the feeling of both love and struggle. Despite it, we held hope in our eyes like song sparrows skimming water, caught butterfly wingbeats at the backs of our throats, and spoke wishes to the hovering flakes of twirling salt departing from land. I couldn't resist going back to that night. The same girls then—different now. So much faith we had.

*

Heavy Feet:

It's occurred to me that never has holding on and moving forward seemed to mean so much. There are bridges I am crossing that don't exist on a map, and I'm still stuck daydreaming about what the earth feels like past a state line. Life here is gold, drives where I could cup the tops of tree yards. Prairie dried stretches heating highway. Doubt, you stole me, but I will always be more brush country and vacant road. More giving than running away. More falling apart than together. More quiet than loud. Needing both to move and stay.

Candy Lips

If you want me—
Don't provoke a fantasy for some wholly formed pleasant thing.
There are days when my lashes, spooled in black themes, are not
for your sake darling, but merely to hide graveyard shades from
tired, teary eyes. Are they not bright enough for you? Don't label
me a bitch because my face, which rests on thinning levels of
contentment, bores you. If interested, catcalling won't do. And
you, blind to the far reaches my life has held, leading to that one
day you caught me off guard when I was breaking, told me how I
should look happy, act lively, be fascinating, sexy, and appeasing.
Fix what you found dull. I'm too exhausted to be anything other
than what I am. And I'm learning that is more powerful than your
definition of stunning. You could have just said hello.

Womanhood

We left our bravery in mantras that deepen with growth. Arms that cradle and endure, bodies that cope. Strength that carries our survival. Our stories, amid generational shifts and varying histories becoming a cornerstone for female power. May we continue to break the molds that have been formed for us. Our universally threaded voices left as artifacts reflecting all the marginalization women continue to overcome.

Sewing Shop

You lost the touch of buttons, the depth of a single loop round
right with needle on the scent of fabric. Only ringing now in
bottle cap noises from angry men. Needing feathers woven from
the backbone of female heritage. My mistake, not remembering
hope like my great grandmother standing in a canary slice of sun.

The Arts

It's okay to forget you hold brackets of bottle brush woods in your brain, and for a night, depart from foraging. How lavish to deal in hands of palettes that shimmer on smoky eyes like the brocade supply of stadium seating at the theater. You'll once again return to the countryside of billowy, nervous tissue in your skull that's marred by some imbalance, so instead, know a night of paying admission to creativity is vital. Become the girl who lives instead of the one who waits to die.

Winged Dream

There is much you can learn from howling dogs.
Reality sets in at funny times. Truth often comes clouded in
mundane rituals. During the roaring symphony of barks quieting
your mess of a mind.
It arrives early morning around 2 AM while watching the movie
Erin Brockovich. Still believing like you did as a young girl, that
struggling women can overcome fucked up standards. Knowing
that somewhere there are relationships that are built on equal
faults and support.
It appears during the light of day while scouring old Bonnie Raitt
songs. Considering what provoked such beautiful lyrics and how
they were scribed beyond the blues.
It transpires while you're lured to the floor, because standing up
is too much.
It leaves you lying in numb colors.
Most of all though, realizations sneak their way in, crushing
every chamber of your heart, when you least expect them.
The difficult discoveries of others hurt more than any of the ones
latched to me.
For there are letters that will no longer stick to my throat...
And all I want is to remind her that women are worth more than
what he expects you to be.
Remember there are gentleman that roam this earth still.
So shelve your energy for worthier nights, for worthier men,
dear sister.
Cause you are a winged dream.

La Luna in every Stage

When your earth shakes, uncover fortunes from steady ground.

* The Color of Awakening

It was a conjuring, like an old wives' tale spun in the history of southwest fauna. Heavenly hopes sent by way of silken cactus flowers, dipped in milky cream and yellow. Only in the night did they show. As if they feared the weight of heat, the light from day. Every time I passed them, planted between homes, I'd catch how the alignment of moon shined against their petals.

Twilight and tears laying to rest at their feet. In one A.M. hues they found their voice.

And I thought, my...
Those sparks could blind the tremble.

*Tin Bird

You never know what will save you on certain days. The tradition of falling doesn't scar as much anymore, but the unraveling of it all has become lengthier with the closing of day and welcoming of moon. I can't find who I was before and after. Before nights spoke in metal and blue, before I attempted to translate allegories, before there was a there and here, before skipped stone dips and rises decorated my waist, before geography cut divides, before I tried understanding men who didn't understand themselves, before family broke, before I broke (me). It's the same thing with everything, this weighted trajectory. After nights that leave ripples, after words are born to frame, after the after is too far gone to go back and there is nothing to meet such ache.

Storms like Seeds

There will be days you'll want to name your storms. Every mystery that's knocked your breath sideways. Wondering why some deliver like saints in the end and others give such unrest. Weary of which are safe to consume, wanting only those that nourish. It wouldn't be life if things weren't falling apart. Paperback days of lessons pressed between seams and pages for each year like a manual on how to survive the wilderness.

Generations

No wonder we clutch near our hearts so tight.
Palm against beat.
Faith in dark.

Extinction

In the metallic
We washed our weeks' worth of ache,
As
The
boy played the coin machine like it was a savior.

If Life was a Nora Ephron Movie This Would Be a Dramedy

On a weeknight, Belinda Carlisle's Heaven is a Place on Earth
played on an episode of The Handmaid's Tale. I heard it in the
backward pulse of my own sitcom body. Shuddered at the
variables of loss on the screen. It wasn't shock, rather an
expected response, like opening one's self to someone. Like
moving mountains inside, the way Sally pretends to excavate her
glory in exhibition for Harry. "I'll have what she's having," but I
cannot carry the weight of melody on my back and still offer my
frame. Our bodies once as rivers, their posture not broken but
full. How wasteful to misunderstand we could sing with our
voices being heard.

A Memorial

The crows sang they drank all they could of their kitchen prayer

I spent a week at my sister's home after her newborn arrived. I had already witnessed the aftermath of a body in creating the sum of its new parts, held my two older nephews as babies when they were vibrant. They became solar systems. It happens so fast, how we discover the many renditions of oxygen and shrink from the alphabet to numbers; transforming our phoenix skin into a creek of showers.

It's beautiful though—
the way we learn
to sit *upright.*

Gravity is Ruthless

Preserve your lines—
daddy long legs are not a
spirit form.
"Walk like Mrs. Onassis", my great aunt used to say, as she would
imitate the figure with straight shoulders and poised, smiling
face.

We Don't Speak Of

desire as an
un
/
opened
verb on the prick of becoming
a dozen highways
passed through the four legs of this
exhaustion.
I want to tear away its collar,
wear it as a skirt uninhibited on the weekend of my limbs.

Old Tradition

first taste,
don't battle
the
disjointed
space.
blues touch
myself

A found poem—Source: Goldberg, Natalie.
Writing Down the Bones. pg 119

American lipstick

is your unlit mouth—
a prop,
a Hell's Angel,
a *nightgown*
around your
world.
Try.

A found poem—Source: Goldberg, Natalie.
Writing Down the Bones. pg. 151

Pen Pals

I sit with you every day, in the quiet reverse to find my
beginning.
If I told you what I know, it would be to hold these words close.

*

There are times you'll worry you're unlike the rest.
After all, what if your warrior heart is buried in the past.
What if you can never travel with the pack, what if your wild
horse pulse doesn't come back?
The one you held inside when you were young and naïve.
When you swung high in the wind beneath an ancient tree.
When you played under the Texas heat, and fought villains you
could beat,
What if the unknown confidence you held when you were a little
girl never trickles to your smile again?
What if your youth was your savior and the rest all a sin?
Like a chorus you can't forget, these words repeat with no end.
And just when you pray for the heavens to listen, you quietly
hear a familiar rhythm.
One of spunk and courage, of hope and peace, of you are worthy,
just believe.
So, follow the tune of your golden compass, the one buried
beneath your ribs.
And remember the girl you used to be, three years old, happy,
and brave.
Does one ever lose that spirit completely?
The answer you conclude is no.
For the same girl you were then will always exist somewhere
deep within your soul.

Flight

"If dreams were lightening, thunder was desire,
This old house would have burnt down a long time ago...
Just give me one thing that I could hold on to,
To believe in this living is just a hard way to go."
'Angel from Montgomery'—John Prine

I've lost count of the parking lots that told me their siren song.
Cars that became concert halls, bruised from skylines echoing
tiny counties seen in magazines withered and saved.
Age sauntering with revelation.

I couldn't shake Bonnie Raitt's 'Angel From Montgomery' when I
first heard it.
The way it approached like bohemian weather on denim vocals.
Its need to purge cherry faces over dinner and lakes you can't
quite name.
How the loss of innocence is a lifelong tale.

I dreamt of the city and passages that broke routine.
Summer skin too charged for nightfall, ice heart rhythms.
All the places that are being destroyed,
their elements no longer left to be studied or honored.

I'm sure it's beautiful and I miss it, even though I don't remember
knowing it.

Call Back to Speak to a Less Disillusioned Representative

It'll be a short summer and the animals are growing old. If fear had a weight you'd call it your body. I know it sounds terrifying, but I feel another nervous breakdown coming on and I'm too busy watching trash tv.

The prompt said to write about love.

Baking Season

Bedrock doesn't always scream as you dig. Sometimes it lags and is imperceptible.

*

A few weeks ago I watched the movie "Julie and Julia" and was reminded of the first time I saw it. It's strange how a memory can be so clear. It feels like an hour ago and not ten years in the past. I swear a day never sheds its ancient life.

I've been wanting to bake. Stir history into something tangible. Feel the ribbon of hurried arms and bent shoulders through my posture. I miss the heaviness behind its activity and how a soft light always regards a kitchen as its being used. But I've become still, a space of excuses. I'll choose a recipe and worry it's a waste of time and involves ingredients I can't afford. I rarely commit to anything anymore. This is who I've become.

The girl sitting in that theater, all those eras ago, doesn't realize how destruction will continue to relentlessly build within. She'll never predict how it's going to go.

So I determine in this moment, keep lending yourself to just another day. Be moved by stories of women making something out of gaping wants. See if your desire to run can be saved by that half-light you've known since you were a little girl in your great grandmother's kitchen. Protect it all from disappearing. Buy the ingredients. Bake the damn pie.

Smallest of Wild

Things I often forget—
there is movement everywhere, even in the quietest of days, even in
the smallest of wild.

I keep thinking about the rituals we build ourselves to carry us through, how one day becomes day three. The shake of blankets at night wishing to predict comfort, that moment of clarity that slips as fast as you catch it, and how each one adds up to tiny hopes.

These last two months have been filled with literature from different countries that remind me human emotion is far more connected than the difference of culture. How the journey of each life can be expansive even in its simplicity.

March arrived and new traditions began. I've been watching Little Women (the 90's version that I grew up with) these past few weeks. There are too many quotes that I love, but the one that remains are these promising words told to Jo... "Go and embrace your liberty and see what wonderful things come of it." I realized our story can be just as poignant as we find the courage to accept the next hour. The liberty we seek is teeming with meaning as we exist in our small routine. Adventure is a beautiful sentiment, but not every day is meant for grandness. Not every life stretches beyond its seams.

This year I've mentally collected scenes and excerpts that eased each passage to the next. In the book *Paradise of the Blind* the words, "To live with dignity, the important thing is never to despair. You give up once, and everything gives way," left me still and awake in its truth. Maybe while the world around outgrows expecting you to move along too, in this quietness of living, you are already overcoming. And in the unfolding of your story, in the solitude of your own theatre as the neighborhood rooster builds a canyon from its sounds—that is a journey in both its smallness and exaltation. That is your path.

Perennial

On this surviving we extend.
Comediennes migrating behind half kitchen windows in a body
of chores.
Pioneers of making tragedy into humor.
*"Nothing is worth more than laughter. It is strength to laugh and
to abandon oneself, to be light."—Frida Kahlo*

This Dirt

This good dirt belongs to the fruit, to the forests, and to the
corruption done by man;
But
Those thinning as rivers, must arrange their rent.
Must cling like the animals to their dying land.
This good dirt doesn't know it's forbidden to survive by the very
bounty it produced because it was told it couldn't.
This good dirt doesn't know it's being poisoned.
Doesn't know its fruit has been over picked by settlers who
turned a blind eye on a summer day when heat turned to control.
This dirt.

Tumbleweed

There are ghosts left for serpent sheets never crisp enough for
done hair.
The cattle peppered their presence near an expressway
—majestic.
Like them, I cling to what's left of the open roof.

Myths

The night became a pastime. An insect speaking in its loudest voice in a language I couldn't forget.

It's funny how light can transcend eras. I often wonder if it keeps track of its age. Does it watch over its generational life and ask what did I offer, what did I take?

The other night my nephew was swinging, staring at the moon. It made me think of staying outside too late when the edge of day met its horizon, and everything would quiet. I was recently listening to On Being's podcast with Jill Tarter. Her word's "we are part of a billion-year lineage of wandering stardust" stayed with me. The familiar glow of childhood reminding me of the unspoken knowledge that something bigger exists. That we hold on even amid disparity, believing a celestial, holy life prevails. And so my question is, when does that hopeful sigh of astonishment disappear? For a second, I understood how it worked. In a moment of silliness I swung with my nephew. His little arm wrapped around mine while we admired the cosmos, always keeping our eyes on the light.

I learned that in physics they have a unique way of counting... "one, two, infinity" they say. And so with every pull of the wind's movement, I braced my feet against the ground and we flew.

"One, two, infinity..."

It was indigo even in the darkness.

Atomic Living in a Bottle

On certain nights skin howls with old and new punctuation marks and your hair becomes a life of its own, humidity mixed with abundance. Age becomes too stubborn to escape and grace is that one lyric you never knew you needed to hear. I smile because faith was never meant to be clean, it strikes abruptly like heavy laughter round old kitchen tables. Like superstition. Like the voice that bellows "take it all in."

Cuisine

In the fridge was a culture of shame and riot.
What we don't see of crumbling holy.
No one speaks of how holy isn't always aware, sacred is different.
A craving.
A starvation.
A mercy.
I've been listening to Patty Griffin like a forgiveness. My appetite
may feel nameless, but the world is buried in grief, so I pray
"swallow" and wake the numb.
You have a bounty of nourishment.

Blue Ribbon Winner

Lessons in rising—
Fragility sounds like screen doors and unused ovens.
Nightfall rolls out its golden hour. It tastes of homesickness.
Goth gray but glorified.
A story chased long after its conceived.
Lemon days baked in the slipping environment, torn by hands.

Decoupage

I've always bartered in thoughts that buy me time in being my own worst enemy. When I don't feel equipped to be the carrier of my life, I tend to sink so others can breathe. To honor yourself means to decorate your flaws in understanding. I keep reminding myself, "Don't forget to feed your spirit even when you're not hungry." Surrender, regress, and progress, then continue crafting through each dawn.